Desert Critters
Plants and Animals of the Southwest

by
millie miller
and
cyndi nelson

Johnson Books
Boulder

Dedication...

to Scott with whom life is ever an irresistible adventure.

Cyndi

Thanks...

Audrey Benedict,
for sharing your expertise,
your enthusiasm & your friendship.
You helped make this little critter
a desert adventure.

to the folks at
Johnson Books,
especially

Barbara J. Mussil
Richard Croog
Mira Perrizo &
Steve Topping

for your support,
guidance &
abiding patience.

Peter,
for helping
us explore the
wonders of the
deserts. May this
be just a
beginning!

Millie &
Cyndi (Mom)

"Rattler"
Rock

REFERENCES

ARNETT, Ross H. Jr., <u>Simon and Schuster Guide to Insects.</u> New York: Simon & Schuster, 1981.

CORNETT, James W. <u>Wildlife of North America: Deserts.</u> Palm Springs: Nature Trails Press, 1987.

EARLE, W. Hubert, <u>Cacti of the Southwest.</u> Phoenix: Desert Botanical Garden, 1980.

MacMAHON, James A., <u>The Audubon Society Nature Guides: Deserts.</u> New York: Alfred A. Knopf, 1985.

NATIONAL GEOGRAPHIC SOCIETY, <u>Field Guide to the Birds of North America.</u> Washington: The National Geographic Society, 1992.

NIEHAUS, Theodore F., <u>A Guide to Southwestern and Texas Wildflowers.</u> Boston: Houghton Mifflin Co., 1984.

OLIN, George. <u>Mammals of the Southwest Deserts.</u> Tucson: Southwest Parks & Monuments Assoc., 1988.

PRINGLE, Lawrence. <u>Batman, Exploring the World of Bats.</u> New York: Scholastic, Inc., 1991.

SMITH, Hubart M. and Edmund D. Brodie, Jr., <u>A Guide to Field Identification: Reptiles of North America,</u> New York: Golden Press, 1982.

For a close-up view of these desert critters, explore the array of national parks and monuments in the southwest.

There are many other fascinating spots to visit, such as

The Arizona-Sonoran Desert Museum (Tucson) & the Boyce Thompson Southwestern Arboretum (Superior, AZ.)

"Joshua Tree Geo-Kinetic"

by Steve Rieman

at Joshua Tree National Park

North America has four major deserts. Annually, they receive less than 10" of rain & they actually evaporate more water than they get. Three are "hot deserts" which get most of their moisture from rain.
The one more-northern desert, the Great Basin, is a "cold desert" receiving its moisture not only from rain, but from a significant amount of snow as well. It also has a lower average annual temperature.

Initials- M, S, C, GB indicate deserts in which plants and animals are found.

This book dwells mainly on the "hot deserts."

Drawings in this book are not to scale.

Every living thing in the desert must adapt to intense heat & limited water. Some animals avoid the hottest season by migrating or becoming dormant. Some simply seek shade or burrow in the heat of the day. Many are active only at dawn or dusk (crepuscular). Others can store water in their body tissue or are able to get sufficient moisture from food without drinking water at all. Some can even concentrate their urine into crystals.

Plants have evolved different methods of coping. Cacti have fleshy stems (water barrels) for storage, & prickly spines (modified leaves) to reduce evaporation. Some act like accordions, swelling with available moisture or shrinking as water dries up. Other plants complete their entire life cycle in one short rainy season.

Some lie dormant, waiting years for sufficient moisture to sprout.

A few have waxy coatings or dense hairs for sunshield & moisture retention.

Many leaf out only during the rains, while others photosynthesize mostly through their bark. Some bloom exclusively at night.

Hemiargus ceraunus
ANTILLEAN BLUE

MS 20"
PAPER-FLOWER
Psilostrophe cooperi

20"
DESERT MARIGOLD
MSC
Baileya multiradiata

WESTERN PAINTED LADY
Vanessa annabella

MSC 3'
Rarely white, always poisonous

Solanum elaeagnifolium
HORSE NETTLE

Millie

CHIA

Salvia
columbariae

24"

MS

BECKER'S WHITE

Pontia beckerii

We reached our campsite at sunset, put up the tent on a sandy expanse, filled the water bottles & settled in for the night. Glad we brought the sleeping bags. It was cold. After a night of restless anticipation, morning came, breakfast was over & it was getting hot. We moved the tent into the shade of a rock. In all the hub-bub, we had our first "Wow! Look at this!" discovery. It was a fragile lavender flower, brilliant & pristine against a bleak background.

WELCOME TO THE DESERT!

Humidity helps to moderate temperature. The desert is a place of sparse precipitation & low humidity, hence it has great temperature variations.

MS

3'

Amsinckia
intermedia

FIDDLENECK

The absence of moisture allows almost all the sun's rays to reach the ground, heating it to extremes. Then at night nearly all this heat escapes freely back into the atmosphere, leaving the desert bitter cold. The desert is a place of striking contrasts & amazing adaptation, incredible lifestyles & awesome beauty, extreme erosion, sudden flash floods & devastating winds.

MSC
...to 2'

PALE TRUMPETS

Ipomopsis longiflora

It's a "critter" sort of place...

colorful birds, prickly cacti, glorious flowers, ingenious insects, poisonous reptiles, thorny trees & sharp-witted mammals.

It's also a very fragile wilderness. Take care to prepare for temperature extremes, always have enough water & leave only your footprints behind.

Millie

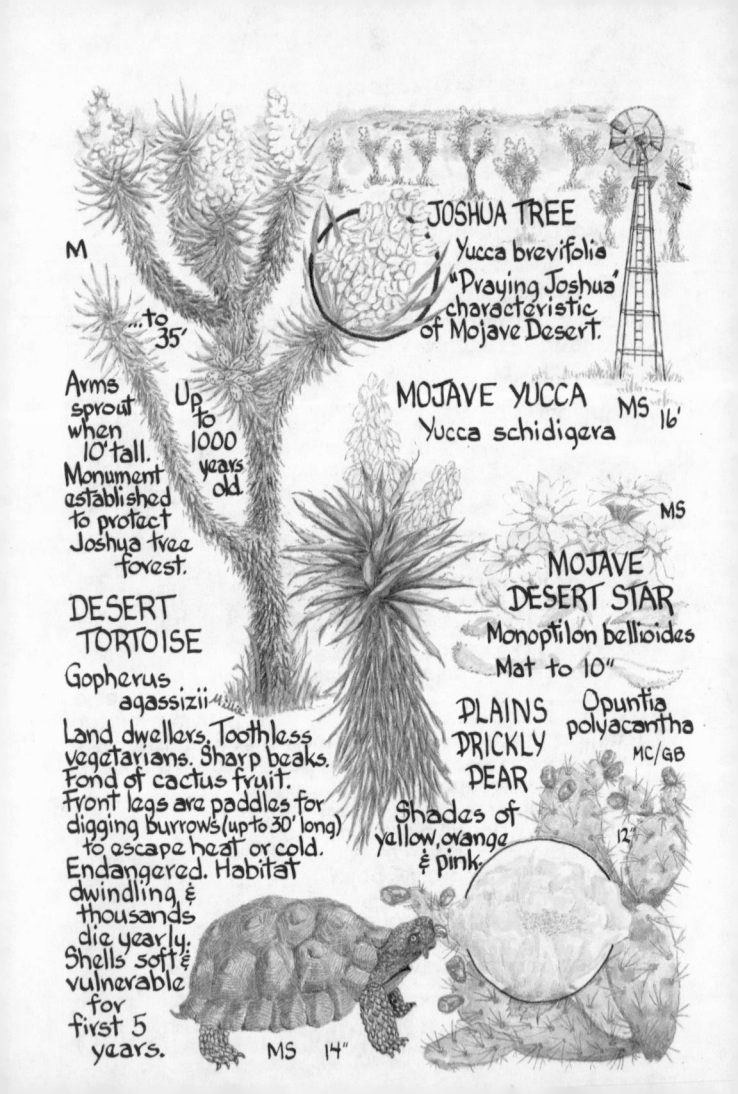

M

...to 35'

Arms sprout when 10' tall. Monument established to protect Joshua tree forest.

Up to 1000 years old

JOSHUA TREE
Yucca brevifolia
"Praying Joshua" characteristic of Mojave Desert.

MOJAVE YUCCA
Yucca schidigera

MS 16'

MS

MOJAVE DESERT STAR
Monoptilon bellioides
Mat to 10"

PLAINS PRICKLY PEAR

Opuntia polyacantha
MC/GB

Shades of yellow, orange & pink.

12'

DESERT TORTOISE

Gopherus agassizii

Land dwellers. Toothless vegetarians. Sharp beaks. Fond of cactus fruit. Front legs are paddles for digging burrows (up to 30' long) to escape heat or cold. Endangered. Habitat dwindling, & thousands die yearly. Shells soft & vulnerable for first 5 years.

MS 14"

RED-SHAFTED FLICKER
Colaptes auratus
Feeds on ground for ants.
...to 12"
MS

13"+

MSC
GB

BEAVERTAIL
Opuntia basilaris

Opuntia fruit (tuna) sought by desert tortoise, white wing doves, cactus wrens, wood-rats, & man (for jelly).

MS

DESERT HYACINTH
Brodiaea pulchella
"Grass nut" bulbs roasted by early folks.
...to 3'

DESERT NIGHT LIZARD
Xantusia vigilis
Velvet skin. Tails easily broken. Fixed, transparent eyelids... always looks awake. Secretive, hiding under rocks or decaying plants. Hunts termites, ants, flies & beetles. Nocturnal. Born alive, tail first.

BRITTLEBUSH MS
Encelia farinosa
"Incienso" used by padres as incense. Sap hard to clean off.
...to 5'

...to 5½" MS

11

Young similar in color to female. Flutters through treetops for insects.

VERMILION FLYCATCHER

6"+
SC
Pyro-cephalus rubinus
♂

MSC
Used for food, tools & medicine.

Prosopis pubescens

SCREWBEAN MESQUITE

Favorite of honey bees.

HONEY MESQUITE

Prosopis glandulosa

Very deep roots help survive drought.

MSC
...to 20'

SC
7½"+
♂

Opens early evening, wilts after sunrise.

PYRRHULOXIA

Cardinalis sinuatus
Bill yellow in summer... never pink.
Eats seeds, insects, especially cotton weevils.

NIGHT-BLOOMING CEREUS

...to 3'
SC

Cereus greggii

Exquisite fragrance. Stores moisture & food in turniplike root weighing 5-85 lbs. Grows near larger trees & bushes for support & protection.

A ball in the shade, "pancake" in the sun. Milky sap. Blooms pink, white, or yellow.
Mammillaria heyderi

...to 6" across

SC

CREAM PINCUSHION

CURVED-BILLED THRASHER

Toxostoma curvirostre

SC

11"+

Bill adapted to dig insects from ground.

Sings from conspicuous perches.

Often nests in cholla.

7-12"

MSC GB

DESERT SPINY LIZARD

Sceloporus magister

Blue patches on males only. Diurnal & wary. Freezes or hides when startled. Eats insects.

MSC GB

SIDE-BLOTCHED LIZARD

Uta stansburiana

4-6"

Most common lizard in S.W. Rocky areas with low vegetation. Voracious appetite for insects, spiders, and scorpions. Bobs head when disturbed.

Singly or in groups. Common in tree/shrub shade.

SC

FISHHOOK CACTUS

Mammillaria microcarpa

10"

Toxostoma dorsale

11" MSC

Seldom flies.

Hides in dense mesquite near water.

Secretive.

CRISSAL THRASHER

13

CATCLAW
Acacia greggii

High grade honey tree to 23'.

Fragrant flowers & devastating claws. Called "wait-a-minute" by pioneers.

MSC

False: "Blind as a Bat." True: Bat vision akin to humans (except for color blindness.)

Less migratory & agile than cousins. Forages on ground for crickets, grasshoppers, scorpions, & beetles, then perches to eat.

PALLID BAT Antrozous pallidus
Most bat vocalizations too high for us to hear except for this fellow.

4-5"

MSC GB

Roost sites include buildings, rock crevices, & cactus cavities, less often in caves. Emerges in dark of night.

I identify by slow wing beat. Moms recognize twins in roost nursery & nurse only them. When alarmed, this bat gives off a skunky odor.

Colored spines form bands

SC to 12"

RAINBOW
Flowers pink to lavender.
Echinocereus pectinatus

GIANT DESERT HAIRY SCORPION
5½"

MSC GB

Hadrurus arizonensis
Ground dwelling. Eat insects, lizards, & snakes. Localized "bee sting" pain is non-lethal to people. Courtship a long pincer grasping dance.

DEADLY. Bite causes immediate intense pain that becomes systemic. GET HELP. Slender. Found under rocks, firewood, logs, etc. Insectivorous.

MS

½-3"

BARK SCORPION
Centruroides sculpturatus

Most SCORPIONS are nocturnal, preyed upon by owls & bats, and hunt in gangs. Glow in UV light. Many have 3 pairs of eyes but hunt by touch. Grasp prey in pinchers, flip tail over to inject paralyzing venom. Thick waxy shell retains moisture. Babes born live & carried on mom's back 1-2 weeks. Don't eat 'til first molt. Then on their own.

VINEGARROON

Mastigoproctus giganteus

SC
1-3"
Harmless,
8-eyed,
whip-tail
scorpion.
Shy & nocturnal
Insectivorous.
When injured, sprays vinegary acid.

S
4-16"
STICKLEAF
Mentzelia involucrata
"Sand Blazing Star"
Clings like velcro.

Sonora semiannulata

GROUND
SNAKE

8-19"

MSC
GB

Many color variations may be found hiding in same rock pile.

Oak & juniper habitat, dumps, & junk lots. Eats centipedes, scorpions, and spiders. Lays eggs.

DEVIL'S CLAW
SC   *Proboscidea altheaefolia*
Creeps to 3'. Dry pod, "unicorn", will grab ankles for seed dispersal. Hooks onto cattle nostrils.

S
to 21'
Spanish for "Old One." Spines long, bushy, & gray when old & bearded.

SENITA *Cereus schottii*

MS
SMOKE TREE

Dalea spinosa

Photosynthesis through bark.

NORTHERN MOCKINGBIRD

Mimus polyglottos

MSC
GB

10"

Eats fruit, berries, insects, & lizards. Very territorial. Phenomenal mimic of bird songs, animal, machinery, even human sounds.

DESERT BUCKWHEAT

3' Eriogonum fasciculatum MS

Many species. Good honey source.

DESERT SPOTTED LEAFNOSE

13-20"

MS

Phyllorhynchus decurtatus

Secretive & nocturnal.

36"
GB
MSC

SNAKEWEED

Xanthocephalum sarothrae

"Broomweed" makes sweepers. Once a snake-bite medicine. Rampant on overgrazed land. Toxic to livestock. Good kindling.

Creeps to 20'

COYOTE MELON

Cucurbita foetidissima

Fruit bitter/poisonous to man & beast (except for one kind of beetle who loves it).

Roots make good soap.

MSC

WHITE-LINED SPHINX MOTH

Hyles lineata MSC GB 3"

"Hummers" of dusk & dawn.

Hillie

SACRED DATURA

MSC

Spreads to 50'

Datura meteloides

Night blooms.

Pollinated mostly by moths. Ants attracted to but discard sticky hard-shelled seed. Poisonous!

REGAL HORNED LIZARD

S

Phrynosoma solare 6½"

Young born alive. 90% ant diet.

Horny "Toad", most active early morning in scrub or cacti. Buries self at night. In morning, pokes out head, patiently waits 'til body warms. Then digs out, raises up on front legs with back directly to sun & basks. "Third eye" on head thought to help regulate basking time. To discourage predators (hawks, shrikes, roadrunners & coyotes) fills up with air 'til huge...or may flatten body, stiffen legs, open mouth & hissssss. Then rocks, jumps forward & even squirts blood up to 4"... from its eyes.

HARVESTER ANT

MSC GB ½"

Pogonomyrmex rugosus

Seed eaters, can severely damage crops. Carries up to 50x own weight in mandibles. Thousands live under conical mound of debris in complex tunnels...thus enriching & aerating soil. Workers can inflict venomous, painful sting.

ANT LION

½"

Excavates cone-shaped well with jaws & hides in bottom. Insects landslide into waiting venomous jaws.

Larvae aka "Doodlebug."

GB MSC *Myrmeleontidae*

17

Falco mexicanus

GB
MSC

Flight strong and rapid.

Wingspan 40"
Length 16"

Spectacular dives to catch ground birds & other small animals.

Fearless fighter, often bold.

PRAIRIE FALCON

Chief pollinator of Chuparosa.

MSC
GB

3½"

BLACK~ CHINNED HUMMER

Archilochus alexandri

Millie

CHUPAROSA

Beloperone californica

Favorite of hummers.
Velvety stems.

MSC   10'

DESERT HOLLY

Berberis trifoliolata

For wine & jelly,
birds & bees.

4½'

INDIAN PAINTBRUSH

Castilleja spp.   MSC/GB

Another favorite of hummers. Tiny root system feeds off host plants.

8"

Quietly searches ground for seeds, insects & berries.

Pipilo fuscus

BROWN TOWHEE   SC

COSTA'S HUMMER
Calypte costae 3"

MS

Felis concolor
MOUNTAIN LION

Solitary, secretive & crepuscular.
Makes "scrape" of leaves or dirt
to mark home boundries...
up to 120 square miles.
Graceful hunter. Stalks & rushes.
Leaps up to 20' to catch prey by neck.
Hunts up to 25 mi/night. Need 1-2
deer/week or other mammals,
birds, even
grasshoppers.
Covers "leftovers"
with leaves or brush.
Wary of man but curious
enough to follow
secretively for
miles. No
permanent
den.

6-20"
OCOTILLO
Fouquieria splendens
Not a cactus. SC
Flowers once in spring.
Leaves only after rain.
Stems root to make
living fences.

Body
5-7'

MSC/GB

18-25"
Lepus
californicus
BLACKTAIL
JACKRABBIT

A true hare.
Life span about
2 years. Solitary,
& crepuscular.
Eats shrubs,

Tail 2-3'

3½"

Tracks

Antelope
jackrabbit has no black
on ears or tail. MSC/GB

greens & cacti. Rests by day in shallow depressions called
"forms". Acute near full circle vision. Bolts 30-40mph. avoiding
predators by zig-zagging. Can leap 20' or straight up,
changing direction mid-air. Nearly transparent ears
reflect light & network of veins dissipate ⅓ of body heat.
Litters of 3-6 born fully furred, eyes open & ready to run.

Smallest US bat, walnut-sized,

& only 1/10 oz. Twin pups born in June.

WESTERN PIPISTRELLE
Pipistrellus hesperus

Day roosts include caves & buildings. Usually first out in evening, identified by slow zigzag flight. Insectivorous & crepuscular. MSC GB 2-3"

Bats are only mammals that fly. Fingers are bones in "handwings." Highly developed hearing & touch. Good eyesight. Use "echolocation" to avoid obstacles & determine distance, speed, trajectory, & size of prey. Due to superstition, pesticides, and vandalism, bat populations are dwindling, & recovery is slow as most have only one young/year. Think of it... one bat can eat 600 mosquitoes/hour.

Millions spend summer in over 24 miles of passages and chambers of Carlsbad Caverns, NM. At sunset, 5-10,000 bats/minute emerge in counterclockwise spiral from mouth of cavern taking 2 hours to leave & forming black cloud 2 miles long. Throughout the night, after travelling up to 200 miles dining on moths & insects, bats dive bomb hundreds of feet back into cavern.

Common & migratory.

3½-4"

MEXICAN FREE-TAILED
Tadarida brasiliensis   MSC GB

8+"

MS

Chordeiles acutipennis

LESSER NIGHTHAWK
Flies low to catch insects on the wing, dawn and dusk.

camile

Flowers open an hour before dark and close midday. Pollinated by long-nosed bats as they sip the sweet nectar.

ORGAN PIPE CACTUS Stenocereus thurberi

S

up to 20'

Found north of Mexico.

Organ Pipe National Monument was created for their protection.

LONG-HORNED WOOD BORER

MSC

1¼"

Dendrobias mandibularis May come to lights at night. Males have enormous mandibles.

PEARLY MARBLEWING
Euchloe hyantis
MSC 1¼"

Male 3/4"
female twice that & carries young on back. Nocturnal hunters with purple eyeshine.

MSC GB
Lycosa carolinensis
CAROLINA WOLF SPIDER

DESERT CANDLE
Caulanthus inflatus
MS 1-2'

DESERT FOUR O'CLOCK
Mirabilis multiflora
Blooms late in day & closes mid-morning.   MSC

to 18"

Catlike Tracks 1¾'
Brushy canyons & open deserts. May be seen by day. Climbs trees for food & safety. Feeds on birds, eggs, small mammals, insects, & fruit.

GRAY FOX
Urocyon cinereoargenteus

Curious, intelligent, and adaptable. Tends to hunt same route, mostly nocturnal.

MSC GB

32-44"

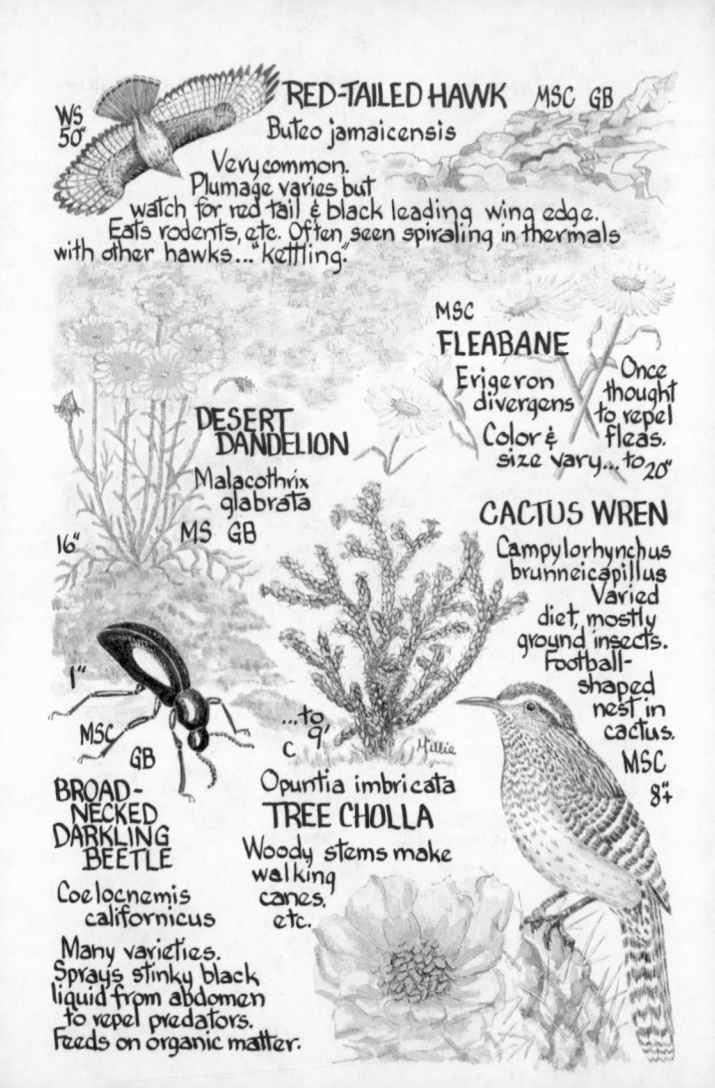

RED-TAILED HAWK   MSC GB

WS 50"

Buteo jamaicensis

Very common.
Plumage varies but
watch for red tail & black leading wing edge.
Eats rodents, etc. Often seen spiraling in thermals
with other hawks... "kettling."

MSC
FLEABANE

Erigeron divergens

Once thought to repel fleas.

Color & size vary... to 20"

DESERT DANDELION

Malacothrix glabrata

MS GB

16"

CACTUS WREN

Campylorhynchus brunneicapillus
Varied diet, mostly ground insects.
Football-shaped nest in cactus.

MSC
8+

1"

MSC

GB

BROAD-NECKED DARKLING BEETLE

Coelocnemis californicus

Many varieties.
Sprays stinky black liquid from abdomen to repel predators.
Feeds on organic matter.

...to 9'
c

Hillie

Opuntia imbricata
TREE CHOLLA

Woody stems make walking canes, etc.

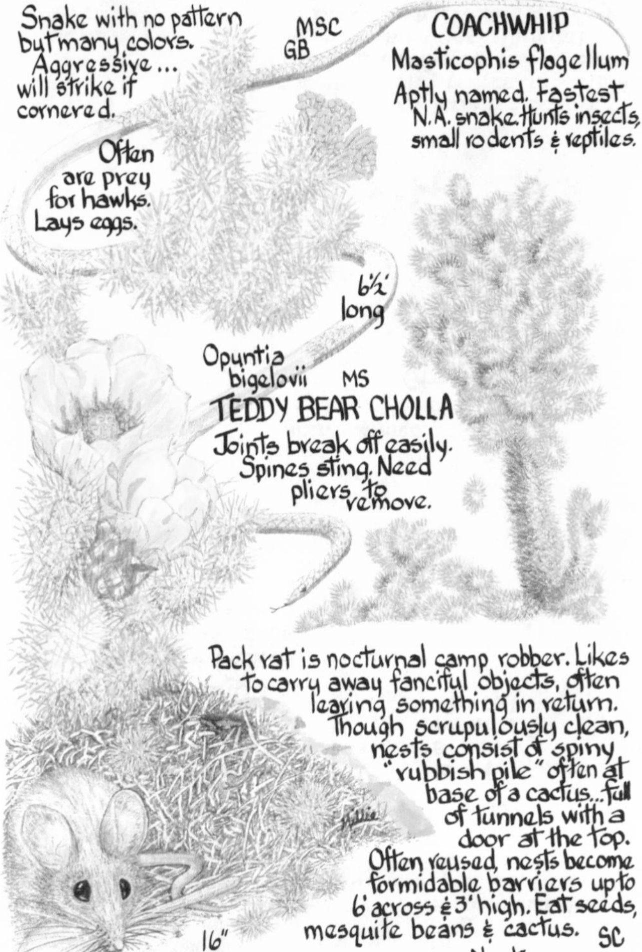

Snake with no pattern but many colors. Aggressive... will strike if cornered.

MSC GB

COACHWHIP
Masticophis flagellum

Aptly named. Fastest N.A. snake. Hunts insects, small rodents & reptiles.

Often are prey for hawks. Lays eggs.

6½' long

Opuntia bigelovii MS
TEDDY BEAR CHOLLA
Joints break off easily. Spines sting. Need pliers to remove.

Pack rat is nocturnal camp robber. Likes to carry away fanciful objects, often leaving something in return. Though scrupulously clean, nests consist of spiny "rubbish pile" often at base of a cactus...full of tunnels with a door at the top. Often reused, nests become formidable barriers up to 6' across & 3' high. Eat seeds, mesquite beans & cactus.

SC

16"
WHITE-THROATED WOODRAT Neotoma albigula

WESTERN SCREECH OWL
Otus kennicottii

Nocturnal.
MSC GB
8½"

Uses tree cavities. Prey includes small mammals and reptiles.

JOJOBA
Simmondsia chinensis

MS
3'

Evergreen. Male & female flowers on separate shrubs.

♂

♀

ROCK SQUIRREL
Spermophilus variegatus

Rock canyons or broken terrain. Burrows beneath large boulders. Food choices change seasonally: spring/greens, summer/fruits, fall/acorns, & winter/stored food for short hibernations. Emits shrill whistle when alarmed.

Ground or rock squirrels gather "goatnuts" avidly. Substitute for sperm whale oil's many uses.

17-21"
MSC GB

GOPHER SNAKE
Pituophis melanoleucus
aka "Bullsnake"

4-8¼'

Very common.

PINCUSHION
Chaenactis fremontii
annual to 2'

GB
MSC

Constrictor. Open, rocky terrain & scrub. Eats rodents. Young prefer insects & lizards. When bothered, hisses loudly, imitating a rattler. Diurnal except when hot. Lays eggs.

MS

BORDERED PATCH
Most variable,
widespread,
& abundant
checkerspot
in the Americas.
MSC

Chlosyne lacinia ♀
1¾"

to 32" **DESERT TRUMPET**
Eriogonum inflatum
Dried stems used
as tobacco pipes.

MSC

POCKET MOUSE
Perognathus spp.
Nocturnal.
Open, brushy, or rocky
habitats. Long leaps on hind feet
resemble kangaroo rat. Plugs up
burrow by day. Fur-lined cheek
pouches carry seeds, greens, or
insects home to eat. Water metabo-
lized from
food.
6-9"

MSC
GB

6"-2' MSC

DESERT SUNFLOWER
Geraea canescens
Pocket mice store
these seeds in quantity.

SAND VERBENA
Abronia villosa
spreads to 3'
MS

WESTERN MOJAVE PATCHNOSE SNAKE
Salvadora hexalepis   Hunts at
midday for reptiles, eggs, & pocket mice.

MS GB
2-4'

25

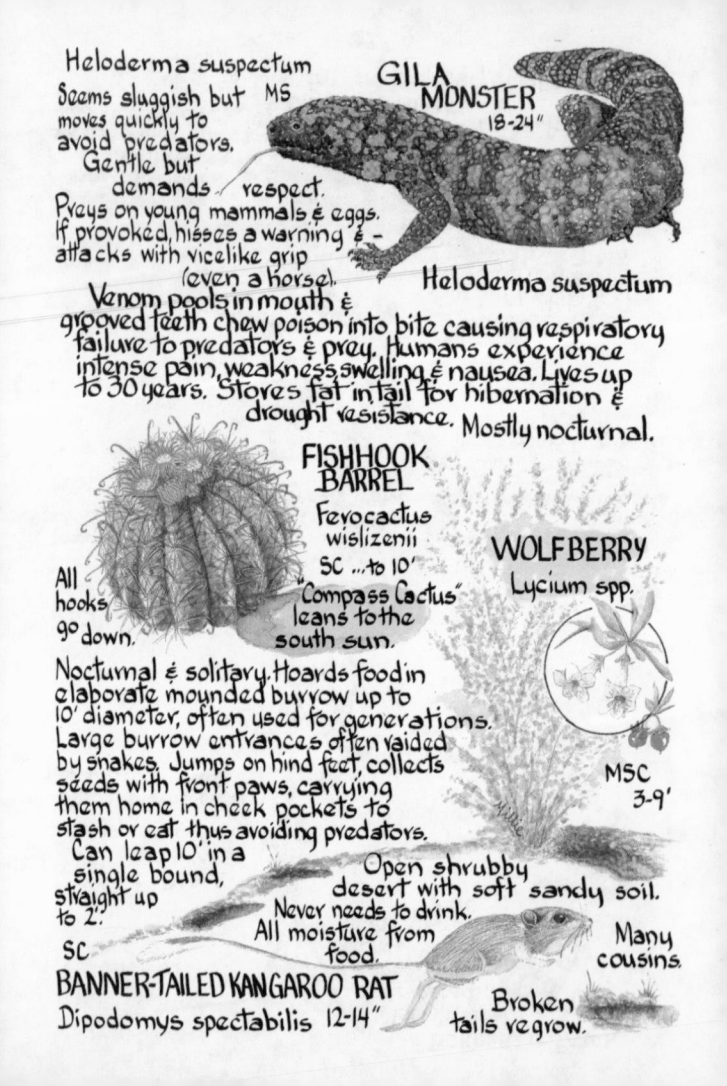

Heloderma suspectum

GILA MONSTER 18-24"

Seems sluggish but MS moves quickly to avoid predators.
Gentle but demands respect.
Preys on young mammals & eggs.
If provoked, hisses a warning & attacks with vicelike grip (even a horse).

Heloderma suspectum

Venom pools in mouth & grooved teeth chew poison into bite causing respiratory failure to predators & prey. Humans experience intense pain, weakness, swelling & nausea. Lives up to 30 years. Stores fat in tail for hibernation & drought resistance.
Mostly nocturnal.

FISHHOOK BARREL

Ferocactus wislizenii
SC ...to 10'
"Compass Cactus" leans to the south sun.

All hooks 90° down.

WOLFBERRY

Lycium spp.

MSC
3-9'

Nocturnal & solitary. Hoards food in elaborate mounded burrow up to 10' diameter, often used for generations.
Large burrow entrances often raided by snakes. Jumps on hind feet, collects seeds with front paws, carrying them home in cheek pockets to stash or eat thus avoiding predators.
Can leap 10' in a single bound, straight up to 2'.

SC

Open shrubby desert with soft sandy soil.
Never needs to drink.
All moisture from food.

Many cousins.

BANNER-TAILED KANGAROO RAT

Dipodomys spectabilis 12-14"

Broken tails regrow.

Smallest fox in NA. Brushy
habitats. Usually nocturnal.
Vulpes macrotis   MSC/GB
KIT FOX

Swift hunters.
Vixens make
permanent
bond with dads
who are excellent
providers for 3-4 kits.
May be seen playing
near den by day.

Rarely drinks
water. Gets
needed
fluid from
food. Furred pads provide traction &
insulation from hot sand.   15-30"

Huge ears
help detect prey & radiate excess heat
from body. Prey includes kangaroo rats,
lizards, scorpions, insects, & birds.

...to 12"
BLUE
GILIA
Gilia rigidula

over
4'

MSC
MORMON TEA
Ephedra spp.
Some grow to large
trees. Primitive conelike
male & female flowers
grow on different plants.
Leaves reduced to scales.
Tasty tea long used as
decongestant &
diuretic.

DESERT
CHICORY
Rafinesquia   MSC
neomexicana
...to 12"

MC

Millie

7-11"
A true creature of the
underground. Colors vary, white to black.
Lives alone, active all year, very territorial
except when breeding.   Digs about 3 tons of
MSC
GB   soil/year, leaving conspicuous mounds thrown from
living chamber. Tunnel systems up to 150' long. Backs out of
tunnel speedily, guided by sensitive tail hairs.
Probes near surface for roots & tubers,
may even pull whole plant into burrow.
Totes food in cheek
pockets so front paws   Thomomys bottae
are free to dig.   BOTTA'S POCKET GOPHER

TARBUSH
Flourensia
cernua
Chewed leaves
taste tarry.
Sometimes used
as a remedy for
indigestion.
"Blackbush" has
black stems &
sticky flowers.
Often with creosote bush.

to 3'
C

♂ GB
MSC
Smallest western
butterfly. ⅜-¾"
Brephidium exilis
WESTERN PYGMY BLUE
♀

**ROUNDTAIL
GROUND SQUIRREL**

8-11"
MS

*Spermophilus
tereticaudus*
Open, sandy desert.
Burrows often
found near
creosote
bushes. Colonial,
shy but curious.
Diurnally active
except during
extreme heat.
Hibernates Oct.-
Jan. In spring, gets sluggish from over-
eating seeds, juicy herbs, & insects.

7-9" GB
MSC
**WHITE-TAILED
ANTELOPE SQUIRREL**
*Ammospermophilus
leucurus*

**CREOSOTE
BUSH
GRASSHOPPER**

Bootettix argentatus
Makes "scratchy"
noise
at night.
1"
MSC

Lives in & eats only toxic
creosote bush. Flies only
when has to. Lays eggs in soil
next to bush. After spring
rain, young hatch and eat
new foliage. Females
mimic old stems.

**CREOSOTE
BUSH**
Larrea tridentata 3-12 feet

Males mimic young
leaves.

MSC

MSC

Oldest known living plant. Requires 120 years to grow 1 foot. One CA plant carbon dated 13,000 years old. Folk to modern medicinal uses. Ten years after nuclear blast in Nevada, 20 of original 21 bushes resprouted at the epicenter.

BLACK-THROATED SPARROW
Amphispiza bilineata
True "desert sparrow." Distinct tinkling call.
5½"

SC

1-2'

WHITE BUR SAGE
Ambrosia dumosa
Grows near creosote. Favorite of sheep & burros. Also red-flowered variety

MS

10-16"

DESERT IGUANA
Dipsosaurus dorsalis
Skittish. Active mid-day, prefers temps above 100°. Climbs into bushes when sand unbearably hot.

MS
Up to 16½"

Darker color when cooler. Basks in morning on large boulders. Stocky, waddles & leaps rock to rock.

Herbivorous (flowers, fruit & leaves).

RATANY

to 24"

MSC

Krameria parvifolia
Common near creosote.

CHUCKWALLA
Sauromalus obesus

cyndi

Inflates to wedge & hide in crevices.

DESERT MILLIPEDE

4-7" SC

Orthoporus ornatus

4 legs/segment. When threatened, coils tightly & secretes repulsive smell. Spends ¾ of year underground. Emerges after rain. Eats mostly dead leaves & bark.

GIANT DESERT CENTIPEDE

9" SC

Scolopendra heros

Solitary & nocturnal. Head & tail look alike. 21 segments, 42 legs. Painful venomous bite to insects, spiders, lizards, small toads, & rodents. Prey held by back legs while hollow front legs whip around, inject venom, & when immobile, eats 'em.

COMMON KING-SNAKE

3-6½'

Lampropeltis getulus

Constrictor. Hunts dawn to dusk. Eats snakes (even poisonous), lizards, birds, & eggs.

MSC

BEAR GRASS

Nolina microcarpa

Many varieties

8'

S

COLLARED LIZARD

SC

Crotaphytus collaris

Males brighter. Pregnant females have orange markings. Eat insects & small lizards. Hide in crevices. Diurnal, territorial, & feisty.

DESERT VELVET

Psathyrotes ramosissima

Strong turpentine odor.

MS

Turtle-like mounds 1' across.

Millie

SAY'S PHOEBE

10"

Sayornis saya

MSC

SC

...to 30'

CENTURY PLANT

Agave parryi

Flowering stalk grows up to a foot a day. Flowers in 8-10 years...then dies.

Nectar to hummers & bats.

Source of mescal and tequila.

Depends on bats for cross pollination.

Likes acorns... plants 'em, caches 'em, & sometimes forgets 'em. Extended family flocks, all help with baby care.

Formerly Mexican Jay.

SC

11"

GRAY-BREASTED JAY

Aphelocoma ultramarina

EAGLE CLAWS SC

Echinocactus horizonthalonius

10"

FENDLER'S HEDGEHOG

Echinocereus fendleri 10"

SC

31

ELF OWL
5½" SC
*Micrathene
whitneyi*
Tiniest of all owls.
Often roosts by day inside saguaro
or other cool cavities, hunts insects,
centipedes, & scorpions
by night.

CACTUS WREN
4-12" MS
*Calliocoris
wrightii*

SHORT-
TAILED
BLACK SWALLOWTAIL
3"
6B SM
*Papilio
indra*

Wingspan 4b
HARRIS'
HAWK
SC
*Parabuteo
unicinctus*

Dove inadvertantly
pollinates
saguaro
while eating nectar. Nest in
mesquite thickets.
Can survive
up to 5 days
without
water.

WHITE-WINGED DOVE
MSC
12" *Zenaida asiatica*
"Who
cooks for,"
you
call
heard
far
away.

GILA WOODPECKER
Melanerpes uropygialis

Female lacks red cap.
Eats insects, fruit, & birds eggs. 9"
Hollows out cavity nest in saguaros. S
Crust forms around hole, protecting against
fatal bacteria. Other birds, rodents, & reptiles
move into abandoned gourd-shaped shell.
When cactus dies, these become "saguaro
boots", once used to hold food.

SAGUARO
Cereus gigantea ...to 50'

Arizona state flower.

Birds disperse seeds.
S

Grows slowly,
branching at about 20',
first flowering at about 50 years.
Blooms without fail. Like many
cacti, accordion woody ribs
allow to swell & shrink with
water. Ribs deeper & waxy on
south side to protect from sun.
Blooms at night. Hungry lesser
long-nosed bat primary pollinator.
Harris hawks nest in crooks of
arms. Sways in the wind.
Often damaged by lightning.

Can live
200 years
& weigh
up to
10 tons

Often sprouts
under "nurse tree"
(palo verde or mesquite).
May outlive its nanny.

...to 3½'

sc

CalNo

Callipepla gambelii

GAMBEL'S QUAIL

Female lacks
black face
& belly.

MSC
10"

FAIRY DUSTER

Calliandra eriophylla

33

LARGE WHITE SKIPPER
Heliopetes ericetorum
MSC GB
1½"+

Bees, wasps, and other flying insects caught on the wing.

Attacks hawks and ravens too close to nest. Common along fences.

WESTERN KINGBIRD
Tyrannus verticalis
8"+   MSC GB

to 3'

DESERT MALLOW
Sphaeralcea ambigua
"Sore-eye poppy" leaf shape varies with water content.
MS

Most widely distributed mammal in U.S. Intelligent, & adaptable.

Hunts singly or in pairs.

Desert coyotes are lean experts in rodent control. Opportunist diet includes plants, jackrabbits, fruit, and insects. Lopes to 30 & sprints to 40 mph, leaps to 14 feet. Can travel hundreds of miles/ night. Commonly yip & howl dusk to dawn. Runs with tail down.

COYOTE
Canis latrans
42-55"
MSC
GB

Mate for years. Often more than one den. Will move pups if disturbed.

to 12"

Tracks 2"
Front

Rear

GB
MSC

COMMON CLARET CUP
Echinocereus triglochidiatus
Flower color varies according to the soil. Often hugs another plant.

TANSY ASTER
Machaeranthera tanacetifolia

to 16"

MSC GB

MORMON METALMARK
Apodemia mormo
Very variable.
C GB 1¼"

TRAILING FOUR-O'CLOCK
Allionia incarnata
"Windmills" spread to 4 feet.
Opens in a.m.

INCA DOVE
Columbina inca

SC
Scrub washes, city parks, & gardens.

Doves feed on fruits.

MSC

In spring, guys "hilltop," looking for gals. After mating, male sips nectar. Meanwhile, female hunts for a tarantula, stinging it to immobilize. Then she drags hefty prey to a grave, lays an egg atop the spider, quickly buries it alive, and leaves larva to feed.

Satisfied, Mom's off to hunt another brooder.

TARANTULA HAWK WASP
Hemipepsis spp.

½ - 4"
MSC GB

Can survive without food 2 years, without water 7 months.

Tarantulas are nearsighted & mild mannered. No web, live in silk-lined burrows. Pounces on insects & small lizards, injects venom, & sucks dry. Sexually mature in 8-9 years. Females live up to 30 years, fellas die after a season of sex. Plugs burrow entrance & goes dormant during times of cold & drought.

6-7"
MSC

TARANTULA
Aphonopelma chalcodes

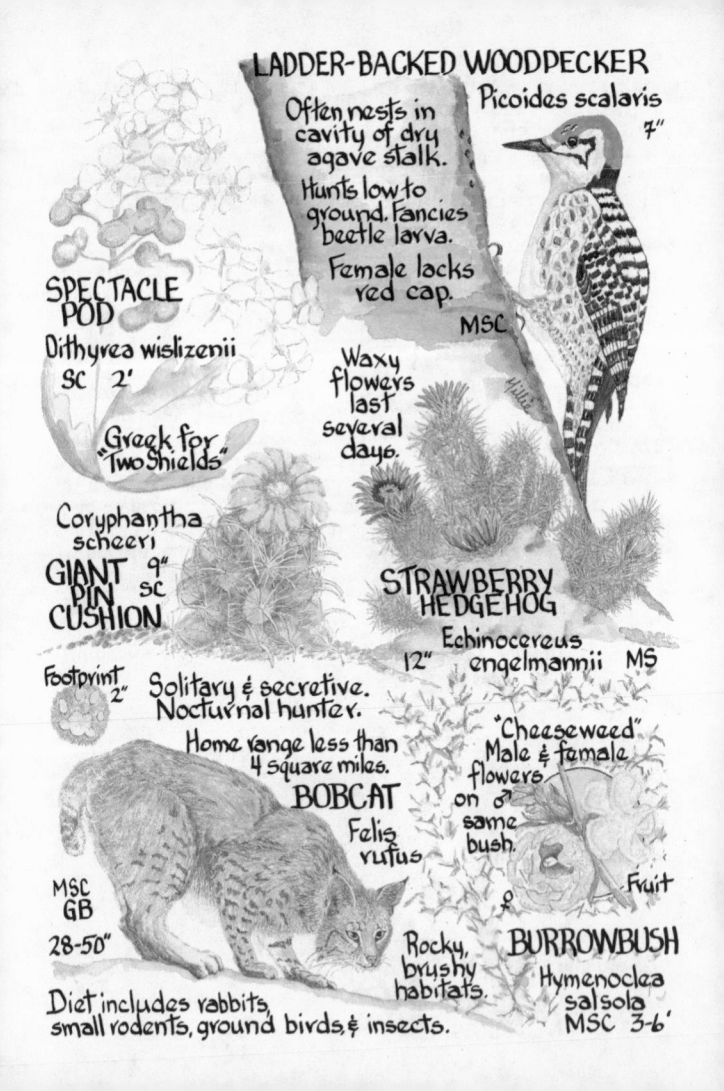

LADDER-BACKED WOODPECKER

Often nests in cavity of dry agave stalk.

Hunts low to ground. Fancies beetle larva.

Female lacks red cap.

Picoides scalaris
7"

MSC

SPECTACLE POD

Dithyrea wislizenii
SC 2'

"Greek for Two Shields"

Waxy flowers last several days.

Coryphantha scheeri
GIANT PIN CUSHION
9"
SC

STRAWBERRY HEDGEHOG

Echinocereus engelmannii MS
12"

Footprint 2"

Solitary & secretive. Nocturnal hunter.

Home range less than 4 square miles.

BOBCAT

Felis rufus

MSC
GB

28-50"

"Cheeseweed" Male & female flowers on ♂ same bush.

♀ Fruit

Rocky, brushy habitats.

BURROWBUSH

Hymenoclea salsola
MSC 3-6'

Diet includes rabbits, small rodents, ground birds, & insects.

DESERT COTTONTAIL

Sylvilagus auduboni

MSC/GB 14-17"

Arrow shafts made from stems.

Prefers briar patches. Seldom ventures into open spaces. A short, solitary life (1-2 years) of narrow escapes from bobcats, coyotes, foxes, snakes, badgers, skunks & raptors.

Relies on zig-zag dash rather than speed for getaways. Rarely drinks, gets moisture from grasses, mesquite, & cactus. Rests in burrows by day to cool off & avoid predators. Blood vessels in ears help give off heat. Several litters a year.

BROOMRAPE

Orobanche ludoviciana

MSC 12"

A parasite.

INDIAN BLANKET

Gaillardia pulchella

"Firewheel" 1-2'
SC

Hibiscus coulteri

SC

DESERT ROSEMALLOW
4'

Millie

When alarmed, raises tail, cha-cha-chas on its hands, & sprays... up to 13'

MSC GB
13-22"

SPOTTED SKUNK

Smallest skunk.
Omnivorous.

Solitary except when breeding or if very cold, when several may share den. Seldom hurry, slow & meandering.

Spilogale putorious

37

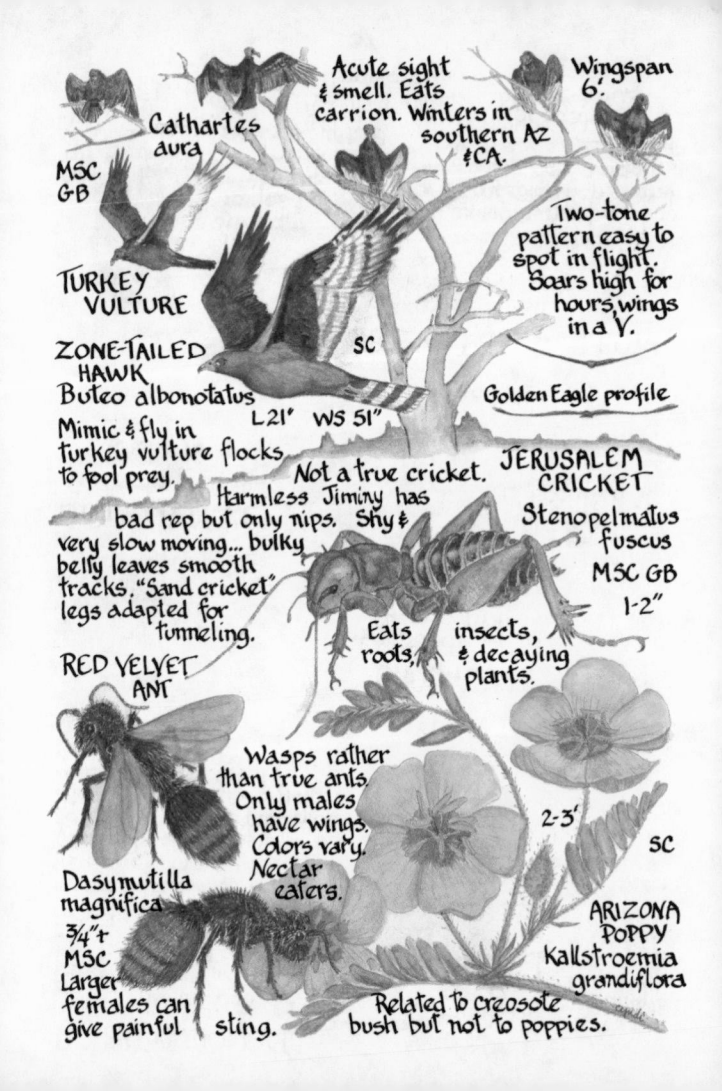

Acute sight & smell. Eats carrion. Winters in southern AZ & CA.

Wingspan 6'.

Cathartes aura

MSC GB

TURKEY VULTURE

Two-tone pattern easy to spot in flight. Soars high for hours, wings in a V.

ZONE-TAILED HAWK
Buteo albonotatus

SC

Golden Eagle profile

Mimic & fly in turkey vulture flocks to fool prey.

L 21" WS 51"

JERUSALEM CRICKET

Not a true cricket. Harmless Jiminy has bad rep but only nips. Shy & very slow moving... bulky belly leaves smooth tracks. "Sand cricket" legs adapted for tunneling.

Stenopelmatus fuscus

MSC GB

1-2"

Eats roots, insects, & decaying plants.

RED VELVET ANT

Wasps rather than true ants. Only males have wings. Colors vary. Nectar eaters.

Dasymutilla magnifica

3/4"+

MSC

Larger females can give painful sting.

2-3'

SC

ARIZONA POPPY
Kallstroemia grandiflora

Related to creosote bush but not to poppies.

LONGNOSE LEOPARD LIZARD   MSC GB
Gambelia wislizenii   8½-15"
Waits in shade of bush to catch
insects & smaller lizards.
If nothing comes   by,
Runs   darts to
at top   another bush.
speed   Color darkens with
on hind   cooler temps.
legs.
      Diurnal.

OWL'S   MS
CLOVER

Orthocarpus
purpurascens

Parasites from
roots of host but   to 16"
makes own
food too.
                    MSC
up to
1/4'   DESERT
                 LUPINE
                 Lupinus
MEXICAN GOLD POPPY   sparsiflorus   MS
Eschscholtzia
mexicana   DESERT LILY
                                Hesperocallis
                                undulata
            to 16"   1-6'
            MS   Bulb
                                   called   (garlic)
                                   "ajo."

                          To avoid heat,
                          cold, & capture, swims
                          under the sand.
                          Has streamlined
               Flaps   jaw for diving.
        over ears, eyes,   5-12" MS
      & nostrils keep out
sand. Fringe on third and
fourth toes of rear feet   Speedy runners
acts like snowshoes on   (up to 23 mph).
and in the sand dunes.
FRINGE-TOED LIZARD Uma spp.

39

GREAT HORNED OWL

Bubo virginianus

Deep resonant hooting. Silent flyer. Varied diet includes rabbits & birds. May be aggressive toward intruders, especially when nesting. Both parents feed young.

Mostly nocturnal.

WS 56"t
L 22"t
MSC
GB

Sociable, small groups widely dispersed in isolated, steep, rocky canyons. Human developments are biggest threat. Rams larger than ewes. 50"t

Never shed hollow horns. Rams' horns take 7-10 years to full curl. Commonly have "broomed" or broken tips, a result of rock abrasion or fighting. To win control of flock, rams run up to 20 m.p.h. & butt horns. The crash can be heard a mile away. May duel for hours, until one gets tired (or gets a headache) and withdraws.

Tracks

3'

Ewes' horns straighter & never more than half curls. Sexes separate except during brief mating season in late fall. Can survive for long periods on dead or dormant plants. Cloven hoofs adapted - concave toe tips catch small ridges with non-skid "crepe soles". Can jump down 20' ledge to ledge. Can spot moving objects 5 miles away.

MSC
GB

Ovis canadiansis
DESERT BIGHORN SHEEP

to 5'

APACHE PLUME
Fallugia paradoxa

MSC

Striking shrubs appear unkempt. Feathery Apache headdress inspired plants name.

HOPBUSH Dodonaea augustifolia

Leaves evergreen, sticky & waxy.

Three-winged fruits more eye-catching than flowers.

S

to 6'

If hiding, snugs tail in to cover white rump.

SC
GB

Tracks up to 3'

WHITE-TAILED DEER

When alarmed, flags white tail & high-tails it.

60"+

Odocoileus virginianus

Only bucks have antlers, which are solid & shed yearly. In spring new antler growth is spongy and velvety. By fall, blood supply is shut off, velvet cracks & bucks rub and polish them on trees. Antlers fall off in winter. Sprints up to 35 m.p.h. Excellent swimmer. Hoofs are main means of defense. Preyed upon by man and cougars. Coyotes prey on fawns, Bucks hang out together.

Does form family groups with fawns. Age determined by wear on teeth not by number of antler spikes. Nocturnal by habit but will graze anytime on leaves, twigs, & bark or tender greens & grasses. Similar to larger mule deer which has "pogo stick" get away, & antlers that branch equally.

aka
Paper bag bush.
Aromatic.

MS

Salazaria mexicana

BLADDER SAGE

to 5'

Commonly found along washes. Showy papery bladders disperse seeds in wind.

41

MEXICAN LONG-NOSED BAT

Leptonycteris nivalis

Not an insect eater but essential pollinator of flowering plants by dining on both nectar & pollen.

Found only in Big Bend, Texas.

"Leaf" on end of nose.

No tail.

3½"

Most bats roost in caves, attics, cliff crevices, & sheltered places. When hibernating, body temperature drops almost to that of surrounding air of roost, but will die if below freezing. Easily disturbed by man, repeated rousing can be deadly as it depletes critical stored fat reserves. Bat quano makes a potent (and smelly) fertilizer.

SCOTT'S ORIOLE
Icterus parisorum

Meadowlark-like song. Often nest in tree yucca. Feast on insects, fruits & nectar.

MSC

8"

Insects only.
MSC

7½"

HOODED ORIOLE
Icterus cucullatus

Oriole female & young are olive-green.

FILAREE STORKSBILL
Erodium cicutarium

Harvester ants store seeds & kangaroo rats eat 90% of seed crop. Seeds spiral selves into ground.

Creeper to 12"

Megathymus yuccae   MSC

YUCCA GIANT SKIPPER

2½"

Soaptree   Torrey   Banana

MSC

LOGGERHEAD SHRIKE

Solitary. Zealously
guards territory.

MSC
GB

Eats
insects,
rodents,
snakes,
or small
birds.

Similar
colors
to the
mocking-
bird.

9"

*Lanius
ludovicianus*

Since shrike
lacks talons,
impales prey
on thorns, yuccas,
or barbed wire to hold
while eating or to cache.

All yuccas are in lily family &
are evergreen. (Agaves
bloom & die) Broad-leaf yuccas
called Spanish bayonet/dagger.
Animals graze on young flowers.
Woodrats eat leaves & use for roots.
Javalinas tear 'em up and
eat their hearts out.
Nighttime perfume attracts
bats &
moths.

SC
17'

13'
C

TORREY
YUCCA

SOAPTREE

Yucca elata

Roots for soap.
Flowers for food.
Leaves for weaving.

*Yucca
torreyi*

Untidy
looking.

Each species
has specific
moth it
depends on
for
pollination.

BANANA
YUCCA

Millie

*Yucca
baccata*

5'

MSC

Fruit... 10"
long & edible.

EVENING PRIMROSE
Oenothera deltoides
MS to 12"

Dried stems
form
birdcage.

DESERT
MARIPOSA

4-8"

Calochortus
kennedyi

MS GB

Also in yellow & orange.

Wide white

bands.

SIDEWINDER 17-33"
Crotalus cerastes MS

Sidesteps...adaptive &
cooler travel for hot, loose
sand. Leaves J-shaped
tracks.

Open
scrub.

"Horns"
fold
down to
protect eyes
from sun and
blowing sand.
Highly
toxic
venom.

Defensive
& quick
to strike.

Extremely
toxic venom.   2-4¼'

22"t MSC

MOJAVE RATTLER
Crotalus scutulatus

MSC

ROADRUNNER

Geococcyx
californianus

Seldom flies. Runs
up to 15 mph after insects,
reptiles, birds, rodents, and even rattlesnakes.

WESTERN DIAMONDBACK
Crotalus atrox
SC Up to 7'
Brushy, rocky places. Second largest rattler. Hunts rodents.

Bands encircle tail. Very bold & less secretive.

Spreading herb to 1'.

PURPLE   SC
GROUNDCHERRY
Physalis lobata

BLACKTAIL RATTLER
Crotalus molossus
SC 2-4' Difficult, mountainous terrain. Fairly unaggressive. Prefers small rodents. Young ones eat lizards.

Rattlers are poisonous. Distinctive broad triangular heads. Heat-sensing pits behind nostrils detect minute temperature differences. Can locate prey in total darkness. Nocturnal in summer. Young can survive on their own immediately after birth. May hibernate in groups. Rattle first a horny "button." Add on as shed (up to 5 x yr.). Old buttons may break off. Rattle sounds like insects or dry leaves. Sometimes rattles before striking. Jaws open almost 180°. Hollow fangs fold out to release controlled amount of venom, some bites are dry. If bitten, KEEP CALM, slows venom spread. Lower bite below heart. If venom injected, hurts & swells quickly. GET HELP!

45

BLUE GROSBEAK 7" MSC
Guiraca caerulea
Nests in thickets.
Especially
fond of
grass-
hoppers.

DESERT TOBACCO
Nicotiana glauca

Tree to 20'+
Poisonous
to
livestock.

MSC

Flowers
inconspicuous.
In fall, seeds
"snow" into
drifts.

SC

DESERT BROOM ...to 5'+
Baccharis sarothroides
aka Seepwillow.
Leafless.

FLOWERS

SEEDS

Tiny, ½ to 1½"
round.
Epithelantha
micromeris
BUTTON
CACTUS

SC

DODDER
Cuscuta indecora
A parasite. SC
Rootless and leafless. Twines around
host like a vine. Plants yield yellow dye.

PHAINOPEPLA
Phainopepla nitens
Likes berries, insects, & mistletoe.
MSC

♂

7"

♀

Often 2 nests close together. Inside stuffed with leaves & feathers. Large one for nesting, small one for dad.

MSC

S
...to 30'
Blue-green bark. Upper flower petal spotted red. Found in washes.

BLUE PALOVERDE
Cercidium floridium

Paloverdes, aka "Greenwood," live 300-400 years. Photosynthesis mostly thru bark where chlorophyll stored. Depend on digger bees for pollination.

VERDIN
Auriparus flaviceps

4"

YELLOW PALOVERDE
...to 25' MS
Cercidium microphyllum
Yellow-green bark. Each blossom has a white petal. Found in foothills.

DESERT MISTLETOE
MSC
Phoradendron californicum

Parasite roots go into vascular system of tree for water, sometimes even killing host. Interdependent with phainopeplas who eat berries & leave seeds in scat on branches. Often protective site of verdin nest.

DIGGER BEES
Centris spp.
S
Nest in ground & emerge when paloverdes blossom.

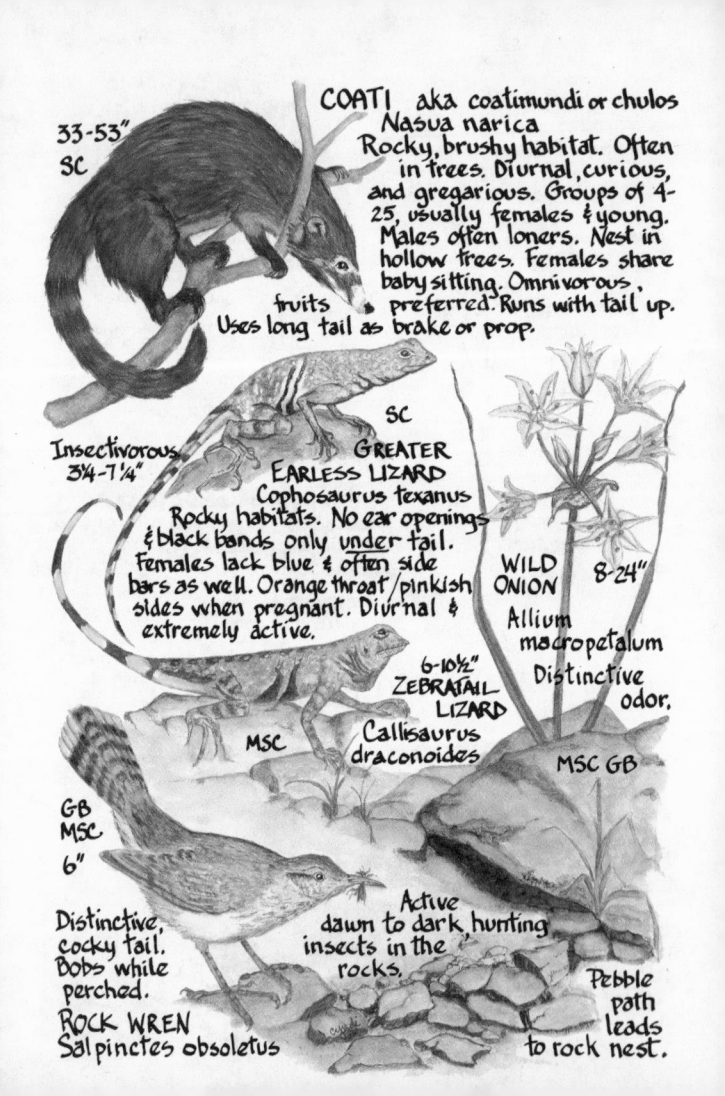

COATI aka coatimundi or chulos
Nasua narica
33-53"
SC
Rocky, brushy habitat. Often in trees. Diurnal, curious, and gregarious. Groups of 4-25, usually females & young. Males often loners. Nest in hollow trees. Females share baby sitting. Omnivorous, fruits preferred. Runs with tail up. Uses long tail as brake or prop.

Insectivorous
3/4-7 1/4"
SC

GREATER EARLESS LIZARD
Cophosaurus texanus
Rocky habitats. No ear openings & black bands only under tail. Females lack blue & often side bars as well. Orange throat/pinkish sides when pregnant. Diurnal & extremely active.

WILD ONION
Allium macropetalum
8-24"
Distinctive odor.

6-10 1/2"
ZEBRATAIL LIZARD
Callisaurus draconoides
MSC

MSC GB

G-B
MSC
6"

Distinctive, cocky tail. Bobs while perched.
ROCK WREN
Salpinctes obsoletus

Active dawn to dark hunting insects in the rocks.

Pebble path leads to rock nest.

LONGNOSE SNAKE
Rhinocheilus lecontei

22-41"
MSC
GB

Nocturnal & secretive. Color variations with white belly. Eats small mammals, reptiles, & eggs. If captured, hides head in coils, vibrates tail, discharges bloody fluid & poop.

WESTERN CORAL SNAKE
Micruroides euryxanthus Poisonous.
"Chews" venom into victum... usually other snakes. Glossy bands encircle pencil-thin bodies.
"Red to black, Venom lack
Red to yellow (white), Kill a fellow."
In defense, buries head under coiled body, waves & strikes with tail.

13-21"
SC

Shy, secretive, & nocturnal.

DESERT SHREW
Notiosorex crawfordi

MSC

3½"

BLUE CURLS
Phacelia congesta

to 3'
MS
"Wild Heliotrope"

Smallest & least known of all desert mammals. Nervous, secretive, & fierce. Battles much larger rodents. Gets moisture from soft innards of insects. High metabolic rate requires nearly constant foraging. Dies in a few hours without food.

8+"

COMMON POORWILL
Phalaenoptilus nuttallii

MSC
GB

Common near roadsides, nests on the ground.

"The sleeping one" takes long winter naps, unseen in the rocks. Insects & water taken on the wing.
Melancholy call "poor-will".

CACTUS MOUSE
Peromyscus eremicus

MSC 7-8½"

Nocturnal & secretive. Nests in rocks & cacti. Tolerates heat & lack of water better than most cousins. Eats seeds & nuts.

49

CLIFF SWALLOW
MSC GB

Hirundo pyrrhonota

5"

8-25'

Eats swarming insects.

Large colonies build mud nests on cliffs, bridges & barns. Return from the tropics mid-March.

DESERT WILLOW
MS

Chilopsis linearis

MSC/GB

Total 30"
Tail 15"

RINGTAIL

Bassariscus astutus Nocturnal, solitary, & secretive. Agile climber uses tail for balance. Climbs high in trees for food or safety. Preys on birds, insects, small mammals, & plants.
Prefers rocky canyons near water. Hind feet reversible. Can do handstands to change direction on a ledge. Young raised by mom & dad. Once kept as pets to rid mines and cabins of rodents.

Raccoon family. Aztec name cacomixtle means "half mountain lion"

QUEEN B'FLY
Danaus gilippus

MSC/GB 5'

2-3" MSC **RED-SPOTTED TOAD**

Only NA toad that lays huge load of eggs on pool bottom... one at a time!

Secrets toxic fluid when eaten.

Bufo punctatus

Asclepias erosa
DESERT MILKWEED

Phragmites communis

RIVERCANE

Bufo alvarius
COLORADO RIVER TOAD

Nocturnal. Breed in rain.
Some anxious suitors
even arrive
before there
are pools for
the eggs.

Eat insects,
spiders, and
S lizards. 3-7"

WILD RHUBARB
Rumex hymenosepalus

Found
along
the
Rio
Grande.
Used
to
build.
Roots
eaten.

COUCH'S SPADEFOOT TOAD
Scaphiopus couchi

Paradoxical...
Live where dry but life
cycle depends on water. Hind feet
dig in backwards, making burrows up to 3'
deep. Dormant most of year. Porous skin
absorbs moisture. As soil dries, shed layers of
skin to form cocoon which reduces water loss.
In spring push toward surface awaiting thunder
vibrations that signal rain. When tremors felt, surface &
head by the thousands to nearest water to rehydrate. Water
absorbed through belly is stored in bladder (up to 30% of weight).
At night, males float in rain puddles & "bleat" for females, heard
many miles away. Thus begins a breeding & feeding frenzie.
Gorge on termites also brought out by rain. Each dawn,
they burrow & wait for evening to party. Eggs can hatch in
36 hrs., & tadpoles transform before puddles
evaporate (2-6 weeks). Then it's back underground.
Feasting will last them 'til next
year's rain & orgy, up to 2
years if no rain.

Eurema nicippe

SLEEPY ORANGE

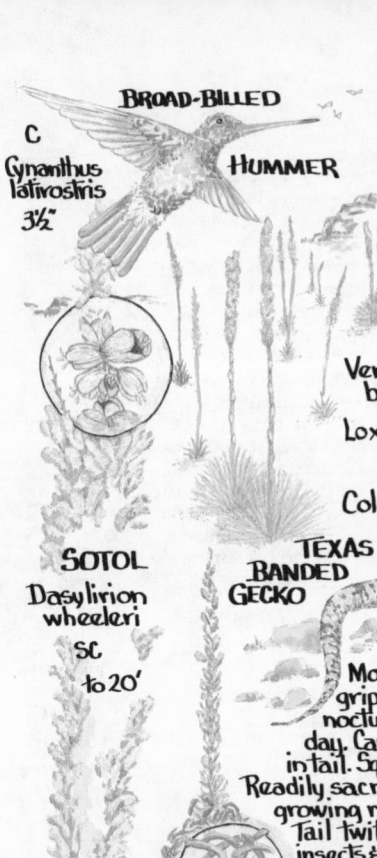

BROAD-BILLED

C

HUMMER

*Cynanthus
latirostris*

3½"

Millie

**BROWN
RECLUSE
SPIDER**

C

5/16"

Venomous
bite.

*Loxosceles
reclusa*

*Coleonyx
brevis*

**TEXAS
BANDED
GECKO**

C

SOTOL

*Dasylirion
wheeleri*

SC

to 20'

Soft
translucent skin.

Moveable eyelids. Toe pads
grip walls & ceiling. Mostly
nocturnal. Seeks shelter by
day. Can survive off fat stored
in tail. Squeaks to communicate.
Readily sacrifices tail when threatened,
growing new one in only 7 weeks.
Tail twitching, geckos stalk
insects & spiders in a catlike
fashion, even wash face with
tongue after
meal.

LIVING ROCK C
CACTUS

*Ariocarpus
fissuratus* flat to 6"

LECHUGUILLA
Agave lecheguilla
Stores food up to 15 years, then flower stalk starts rapid growth. Needle-like tips cause painful wounds & slash legs of horses and cattle.

...to 15'

C

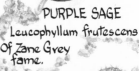

C

PURPLE SAGE
Leucophyllum frutescens
Of Zane Grey fame.

Echinocereus viridiflorus
...to 8"

C

GREEN-FLOWERED RAINBOW

C

SCALED QUAIL
Callipepla squamata
Fast runners.
9"+

2x3"

PEYOTE
C

Lophophora williamsii

53

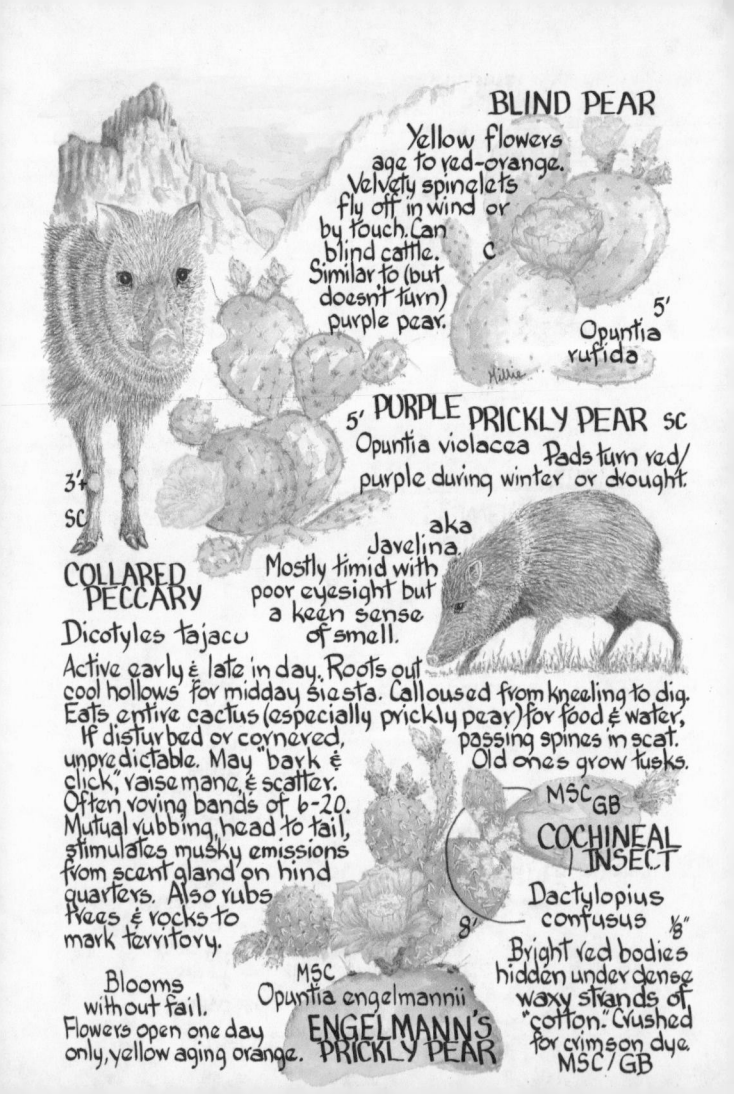

BLIND PEAR

Yellow flowers age to red-orange. Velvety spinelets fly off in wind or by touch. Can blind cattle. Similar to (but doesn't turn) purple pear.

C

5'

Opuntia rufida

Killie

5' **PURPLE PRICKLY PEAR** sc

Opuntia violacea Pads turn red/purple during winter or drought.

aka Javelina. Mostly timid with poor eyesight but a keen sense of smell.

3'

sc

COLLARED PECCARY

Dicotyles tajacu

Active early & late in day. Roots out cool hollows for midday siesta. Calloused from kneeling to dig. Eats entire cactus (especially prickly pear) for food & water, passing spines in scat. Old ones grow tusks.

If disturbed or cornered, unpredictable. May "bark & click," raise mane, & scatter. Often roving bands of 6-20. Mutual rubbing, head to tail, stimulates musky emissions from scent gland on hind quarters. Also rubs trees & rocks to mark territory.

MSC GB

COCHINEAL INSECT

Dactylopius confusus ⅛"

Bright red bodies hidden under dense waxy strands of "cotton." Crushed for crimson dye. MSC/GB

Blooms without fail. Flowers open one day only, yellow aging orange.

MSC

Opuntia engelmannii

ENGELMANN'S PRICKLY PEAR

8'

S

...up to 30'

Overused as firewood.

DESERT IRONWOOD
Olneya tesota

BLACK-TAILED GNATCATCHER
Polioptila melanura

4½"

MSC

Usually appears
lifeless. Lives
400-700 years.
So hard & heavy,
sinks in water.
Seeds & pods eaten by javalina,
pocket mice, & woodrats.
Some say seeds taste like
peanuts. Mistletoe causes
tumorlike swellings up
to 3' diameter &
400-800 pounds.

...to 12"

PORCUPINE
Opuntia erinacea
Red, pink, or yellow blooms.

MS
GB

FLAT-TAIL HORNED LIZARD

Habits
similar
to the
Regal. Diurnal.
Only horned lizard
with dark line
down back.

Millie

Prefers
sandy areas with
sparce vegetation.

S

3-5"

Phrynosoma m'calli

...to 3'

MSC/GB

Grows in chains along ground. Settlers used as cattle food.

BROWN-SPINED PRICKLY PEAR   *Opuntia phaeacantha*

55

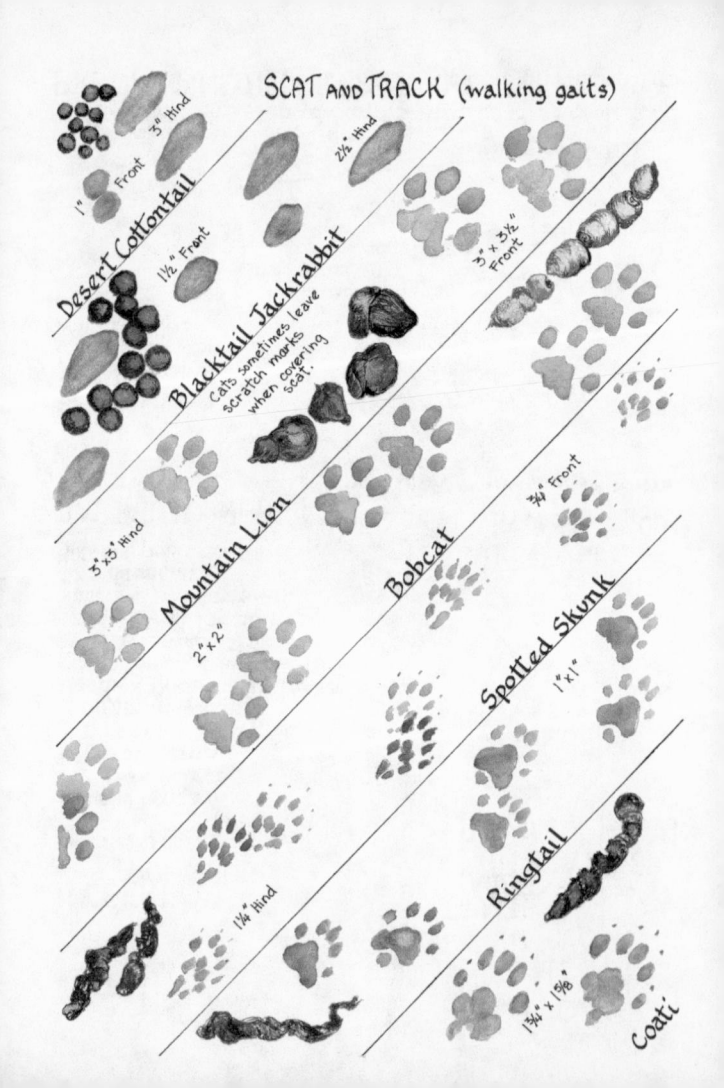

SCAT AND TRACK (walking gaits)

Desert Cottontail — 1" Front, 3" Hind

Blacktail Jackrabbit — 1½" Front, 2½" Hind, 3" x 3" Hind

Mountain Lion — 3" x 3½" Front, Cats sometimes leave scratch marks when covering scat.

Bobcat — 2" x 2"

Spotted Skunk — ¾" Front

Ringtail — 1" x 1", 1¾" Hind

Coati — 1¾" x 1⅝"

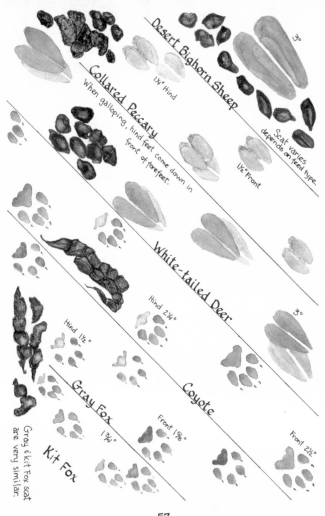

Desert Bighorn Sheep

1¼" Hind

3"

Scat varies depends on feed type.

Collared Peccary

When galloping, hind feet come down in front of forefeet.

1½" Front

White-tailed Deer

Hind 2¼"

3"

Hind 1½"

Coyote

Gray Fox

1¾"

Front 1⅝"

Front 2½"

Kit Fox

Gray & kit Fox scat are very similar.

57

Field Notes

ASH-
THROATED
FLYCATCHER   MSC
Myiarchus cinerascens

ANIMALS

MSC GB

COMMON RAVEN
Corvus corax   24"†

Omnivorous, but eats mostly carrion. High I.Q. Roost by the hundreds in winter. Spectacular courtship. Mates for life.

DESERT HACKBERRY
Asterocampa leilia

PLANTS

CINCHWEED   MSC
to 8"
Pectis papposa

Carpets sandy flats after rains. Heavy lemon or caramel odor, exuded from orangish oil glands. Once used as food seasoning and body perfume.

MSC/GB

Creeps to b

PURPLE MAT

Nama demissum